Harpoon
of the
Hunter

Harpoon of the Hunter

by Markoosie

illustrations by
Germaine Arnaktauyok

McGILL-QUEEN'S UNIVERSITY PRESS
MONTREAL & KINGSTON • LONDON • BUFFALO

©1970 McGill-Queen's University Press
First published 1970
Reprinted 1971, 1974, 1976, 1982, 1990
First published in paperbound edition 1974
Reprinted 1976, 1982, 1990, 1994
ISBN 0-7735-0102-9 (cloth)
ISBN 0-7735-0232-7 (paper)
LC 73 138463

Design by
Ib S. Kristensen

PRINTED IN CANADA

FOREWORD

To SOUTHERN EYES, the setting of this book is a barren land, a lunarscape of snowswept black rocks and of sea-ice wracked into a wilderness of strange and jumbled dolmens and pressure ridges. But there is life hidden everywhere, bird, animal, and marine life, and human life depending on the rest for its survival. This is the land of the Eskimos, the timeless wanderers who understand it and love it with an intensity shared by no other race on earth.

There are two seasons in this land: a long winter with endless, dark nights, and a brief, bright summer of a few weeks, when the sun shines all night and nature renews itself. Summer is not a time for storytelling because everyone is too busy. Winter, when the snow beats against the windows and the wind hums and howls around the houses, is the time for the telling of stories.

Resolute is the only settlement on Cornwallis Island, and it is home to Markoosie, the author of this story. Like his forefathers, he uses only one name. His wife is Zipporah, and his little son is called Ipellie. He is proud of them and especially of Ipellie, for a son is the extension of the father and the continuation of the Eskimo race, who number only sixteen thousand in all the vast northland of Canada.

Resolute has a small airport and a sign that states it is the 'Crossroads of the Arctic'. A De Havilland Twin Engined Otter often lands on the short landing strip. Markoosie is an arctic pilot. When he flies charter trips for his employer, he is very much aware that he is covering in hours distances that took months when his father and grandfather travelled by dog team.

The past is never far away. When flying over this seemingly trackless land near the magnetic pole, Markoosie sees landmarks known to the eye of every Eskimo hunter. They have names recalling long-ago camps, killing grounds, and meeting places. It is natural for him to become introspective at times and to remember ancient tales and traditions. He advances two steps farther—he creates his own stories and he writes them down.

Eskimo traditional stories and legends are unique, having few parallels in the folklore of other peoples. The language is rich in imagery, a perfect vehicle for the storyteller. Unfortunately, few southerners have been able to translate completely or to commit these stories to writing in such a way that they could become part of the world's popular literature. The late Knud Rasmussen was an exception, but he had learned the language at his mother's knee. Markoosie has the rare ability to tell a story in his own tongue and in ours. He is all Eskimo but, having a good knowledge of English, has a foot in the southern world too.

I had studied the folklore and traditions of the northern people from as many written sources as I could find before going to the Arctic for the first time. But books are usually far different from real life, especially in a fast-changing society such as the modern north. To my great joy, however, I discovered that storytelling is still a real and living art. The older people went out of their way to tell me stories. They were anxious that the legends should not die.

I was excited. Eskimo literature could spring, as English and other literatures have done, from oral tradition. But we had to hurry.

Back in Ottawa, we revived the long-dormant newsletter *Inuttituut* (Eskimo Way), resolving to make it entirely Eskimo in content. Because we could not wait for a perfected writing system, we used the syllabics introduced by the missionaries and used for Bible translations. Because we wanted to publish as soon as possible, we were prepared to carry only folk tales at first.

After the second issue of the magazine had reached its readers, material began to come in—not only legends, but biography, poetry, songs, humour. It was the first step from an oral to a written literature which could reach beyond the circle of the firelight.

Then came our first original story written in Eskimo. When 'Harpoon of the Hunter' arrived we could not hide our excitement. We ran the story as a serial in *Inuttituut*, and we encouraged Markoosie to translate it into English. Here, for the first time, was a story of life in the old days, not as it has appeared to southern eyes, but as it has survived in the memory of the Eskimos themselves.

James H. McNeill
Literature Development Specialist
Cultural Development Division
Department of Indian Affairs and
Northern Development

ᑕᒪᓂᓗ ᓯᑯᒥ ᐊᐅᓕᒋᑐᒥ ᓄᑲᐳ ᑕᑲᐃᓯᓗᑎᓗ. ᑕᒪᓇ ᑲᐱᐋᓇᓗᐊᑐ ᐊᑐᕆᕋᒥᐅ ᐃᓯᒪ-
ᓕᐳ ᓄᑲᑎᑕᐅᔭᓇᕈᓐᑐ ᑭᓂᓂᐊᓂᒥᓂ. ᑕᐹᓗᓂ ᑕᑲᐃᓯᐳ ᓂᕆᓗᕆᓗ. ᑕᒪᓂ ᓕᓯ ᓂᑭᓕ-
ᐅᑎᓗᒍ ᐊᐃᔅ ᐊᐃᐳ ᓕᓯᓗ ᑲᐃᔭᒥ ᑕᑯᒪᒥ ᑭᓇᐅᒪᒪ ᐊᐱᕆᐳ ᑕᑐᒪ ᐃᓕᑕᓯᒋᓇᒥ. ᐊ-
ᐃᔅ ᐊᑎᒥᓂ ᐅᑲᓗᓂ ᐊᐃᐳ ᐊᐱᕆᓗᓂᓗ ᑲᓄᐃᒪᒪ. ᓕᓯ ᐅᑲᓗᓂ "ᑕᑲᐳᒪ ᐊᓯᐊᓗ".
ᐊᐃᔅ ᐅᑲᕆᐳ "ᐋᓇᒧ ᑕᒪᓇ ᐊᑐᕋᔅᐅᒋᒪ ᐊᑐᑕᐳ". ᓕᓯ ᐅᑲᕆᐳ "ᐊᒥᓯᐃᑐᓗᒪ ᑲ-
ᐱᐊᓇᑐᑯ ᐃᒋᕋᓯᒪᒪᒪ ᑕᒪᓇ ᐊᖅᑐᐃᓇᐅᐳ". ᐊᐃᔅ ᐅᑲᕆᐳ "ᑕᐅᑐᑲᑕᐳᒪ ᐊᓇᐅᒪᓗ-
ᐊᓗᑎ ᐊᒍᑎᑐ ᐱᔭᓇᕋᕕ". ᐊᒪ ᓕᓯ ᐊᐱᕆᓕᕆᐳ "ᑲᓄᓕ ᐃᓯᒪᕕ ᑕᐃᑯᐊ ᑭᓂᓂᐊᑕᐳᑦ
ᑕᑯᓂᐊᕈᑎᒋ ᑕᑯᓂᐊᒋᑯᑎᒋᓗᓂ?". ᐊᐃᔅ ᑭᐅᓗᓂ: "ᑲᐅᖅᒪᐳᒪ ᑕᑯᓂᐊᑕᐳ ᑭᓯᐊᓂ
ᑲᐅᖅᒪᒋᓕᒪ ᐃᓄᑎᓗᒋᓗᓂ ᑐᑯᒪᑎᓗᒋᓗᓂ ᑕᑯᓂᐊᒪᒪᑎᒋ". ᓕᓯ ᐊᐱᕆᓕᕆᐳ "ᑕᐃᑯᐊ

ᑐᑯᒪᓇᓯᒋᓕᐱᒋ?". ᐊᐃᔅ ᑭᐅᓗᓂ "ᑕᒪᓂ ᓄᓇᒥ ᐊᒥᓯᒪᑕ ᑲᐱᐊᓇᑐ ᐱᒋᒋᓕᐸᑲ".
ᓕᓯ ᐅᑲᕆᐳ "ᑲᐅᖅᒪᐳᒪ ᑲᐱᐊᓇᑐ ᐊᒥᓯᒪᑕ ᑕᐃᑯᓇᓂ ᐅᒪᔭᓯᐅᑐᓂ ᑭᓂᕆᐊᑕᑎᓂ ᐃ-
ᓕᑲᐱ?". ᐊᐃᔅ ᑭᐅᐳ "ᓄᑲᕋ ᐃᓕᐅᐳ ᓇᐅᓕᒥ ᐊᑎᓕ". ᐊᒪᓗ ᐊᐱᕆᓗᓂ "ᑭᓇᑯᓂᓕ
ᐃᓕᑲᐱ ᒪᓂ?". ᓕᓯ ᑭᐅᐳ "ᐊᑎᕋ ᑲᐅᖅᒪᓕᐸ ᐊᑕᑕᒪᓗ ᐊᒍᑎᒥ ᐊᑎᑲᐳ ᑕᒪᓂᓗ ᑭ
ᑭᑕᔭᐊᒥᐅᓂ ᐊᒪᔭᑲᒍᐳ, ᐋᓇᓇᒪ ᑐᑯᓕᐅᐳ ᓯᓕ ᓄᑕᕋᐅᑎᓗᒪ. ᓄᑲᑲᐳᒪ ᐊᑕᐅᓯᒥ ᐊ
ᓂᑲᓗᒪᓗ ᐊᑕᐅᓯᒥ. ᑕᐃᒪᒪ ᐊᑕᑕᓂ ᒪᓕᐸᐳᒪ ᒪᑲᐃᓕᒪ ᒪᑲᐃᑐᓗ ᐱᖅᑎᐊᓕᒋᓂ ᐊᒍ-
ᑎᐅᓗ ᐱᓇᓯᐊᒪᒪᓂ ᑲᐅᖅᒪᓯᐊᓕᐳᒪ".
ᐊᐃᔅ ᐊᐱᕆᓕᕆᐳ "ᐅᐃᑲᒋᓕᑎ ᓯᓕ?". ᓕᓯ ᑭᐅᐳ "ᐅᐃᑲᒋᓕᒪ ᓯᓕ ᐅᐃᑲᕈᒪᒋᓇᒪ".
ᐊᐃᔅ ᐅᑲᕆᐳ "ᐊᓯᐊᓗ ᐃᓂᑯᓇᕋᕕ ᓄᓕᐊᑲᒋᑯᒪ ᓄᓕᐊᑕᕆᔭᒪᒪᖅᐸᒋ".

A page from the Eskimo version of 'Harpoon of the Hunter', published in *Inuttituut*.

ACKNOWLEDGEMENTS

The author and publisher wish to thank the Honourable Jean Chrétien and members of the Department of Indian Affairs and Northern Development, not only for the financial support which has made publication of this work possible but for the interest and concern which has discovered and encouraged talent among the Eskimos of the Canadian North. Our special thanks go to James McNeill, who brought together author, artist, and publisher. Modest and self-effacing, he has nevertheless inspired us all with his enthusiasm for the project, and has provided generous help and practical guidance at every stage in the production of this book.

THE SOUND OF THE HOWLING WIND
and the beating of snow on the side of the
igloo told them that the weather was too hazardous
to go hunting. The storm had gone on for three sunrises.
Suluk knew that if it did not calm in a few more sunrises
they would be hungry again. He had killed two seals four
sunrises ago when he and his son, Kamik, had gone out
hunting. But two seals do not last long when they have to
be shared by a man and his family and their dogs.

'I guess the best thing we can do today is to sharpen
our harpoons and have them ready for the next hunt.
You will have to help me with them, Kamik.'

Kamik was always willing to help his father at this kind
of work. He wanted to be a good hunter like Suluk. As far
as he was concerned, his father was the best hunter in the

11

whole north country. Suluk had to keep his family fed, but sometimes they had very little to eat no matter how much they hunted. The animals they depended on for food and clothing became scarce with the season. Often nature itself seemed to turn against them.

'I hope we will get polar bear the next time we go hunting, Father', Kamik said hopefully.

'I hope so, too', Suluk said. 'Polar bear meat lasts a long time and the skin is good for clothing.'

Ooramik, Kamik's mother, was chewing sealskin to soften the tough hide; she was hoping to finish new sealskin boots for Suluk and Kamik before they went on their next hunt. Kamik was thankful to have such an experienced mother, who spent all her waking hours working on their clothing. Without warm clothing they wouldn't last long in this country; but with such good clothing they would never get cold even on the coldest day.

Maybe they would be lucky and get a polar bear. But Kamik knew that hunting bear is not easy. He knew that many times hunters come back empty handed after many sunrises of chase, sweat, and exhausting work. Bear hunting is the hardest thing in the north. The bear, if cornered, can kill many good dogs or men, if he gets the chance. But that is life. To survive in this wild land, man and beast kill for food. This is the land where the strong survive. The weak do not survive.

Kamik was learning to be a good hunter. His father had taught him all the skills a hunter needs to know, and Kamik had been throwing a harpoon to improve his aim. Now, at sixteen, he was almost as good as a man and felt he was ready to go as one of the hunters. Many times

Kamik had heard how his father once killed a bear single-handed. Suluk had been lucky, for, though the bear had thrown him, he had managed to get his harpoon through the bear's heart. He had not been able to walk for many sunsets and sunrises. Now he walked with a limp. But to Kamik he was still the best hunter in the north.

THAT NIGHT, AS KAMIK LAY AWAKE, tragedy struck. Suddenly the silence was disturbed by the sound of dogs howling. Kamik woke his father, who was sleeping soundly. Suluk wasted no time putting on his clothing and was outside before Kamik could put on his boots. As Kamik stuck his head out, he stopped in horror. There in front of Suluk was a great white bear. He saw his father reach for the harpoon, but the bear was fighting dogs and paid no attention. Suluk aimed and threw, and the harpoon struck the bear in its hind leg. The bear roared and jumped away from the dogs. As quickly as it had come, it disappeared. All this time Kamik had not moved. He was paralysed with fear and had frozen in his tracks. Now he was ashamed of himself. Maybe he was not ready to become a hunter yet, he thought.

The other hunters began to arrive with harpoons in their hands. They were too late. The bear was gone, but it had left five dead dogs. The hunters looked at the dogs and the sight made them sick. Some had their stomachs torn open, some their legs torn off. One dog's throat was torn open, on another every organ showed. The snow was covered with blood.

13

Later his father told the hunters that the bear had acted strangely. From his many experiences with bears, he could tell that it was not right in its mind. Even a bear will not come to a settlement just to fight the dogs. The one that had attacked tonight was, he thought, mad. This sickness had struck before, but only in foxes and dogs as far as he could recall. Suluk was sure that the bear had rabies. A bear with rabies could be the most dangerous animal to walk this land. If it fought with other bears, then they would get rabies too. Nothing would be safe. That night it was decided that the bear would have to be killed at all costs. It must be tracked and killed, and soon. The hunters decided they would start hunting for the bear next daylight.

'I want all the men I can get', said Suluk. 'If we find the bear again, which we must, this will be the most dangerous hunt you have ever been on. Anyone who does not wish to go, say so.'

Kamik wanted to say that maybe he was not fit to be called a hunter yet; he had acted in a cowardly way while his father fought the bear alone. But he couldn't find his voice.

'Very well,' said Suluk, 'we will start at the first sign of dawn, stormy or not. I want Issa and Mittik to stay in the settlement to look after the people here and protect them against any danger that may arise while we are gone. I want everyone to understand that we may be gone for a long time, and there is always the possibility that some of us may not come back from this hunt.'

Next day the wind was calm, but it was cold. All the hunters except Mittik and Issa began to get ready for the

14

trip, each man thinking his own thoughts. Maybe some of them were wondering if they would ever come back alive. Kamik helped his father harness the dogs. His mother, Ooramik, was tying supplies to the sled. At last everyone was ready, and at the sound of snapping whips the dogs let out a howl and jumped forward. Kamik and Suluk waved to Ooramik in farewell. Ooramik, who was standing beside their igloo, waved back. She knew her loved ones once again faced danger, as they had countless times before. But this time would be the most dangerous hunt of all.

'Why don't they just leave the bear alone?' she asked herself. But she knew the answer. If that bear was not killed, it would endanger the whole north country, and sooner or later it would attack again. She started for the door but stopped. Once again she looked at the hunters, who were now far off. She looked, as though she would never see her loved ones again. She tried to tell herself that everything would be all right, but deep down she had a feeling something terrible would happen before this hunt was over.

FROM WHERE HE SAT ON THE SLED, Kamik could see what had happened last night. A dog with its belly torn. Another with its leg torn off. It was a sorry sight. He felt a little scared. But knowing that he was one of the hunters now he felt a little better, and told himself he would try his best to earn the name. There were nine men and sixty dogs; and the men were experienced hunters who

15

had faced a thousand dangers from beasts, hunger and sickness, and the fury of nature. With these hunters, Kamik thought, they would have every chance to get that bear. But one thing was certain. If they met the bear, some of these dogs and maybe some of these brave men would feel its anger. But how many? And when? Only time could tell.

The island would be the place to start looking for the first sign of bear. When they got there, the storm had buried all signs and tracks, but from experience the hunters knew that this was where many young cubs were raised, and this was a place where they had seen and killed many bears. The day was old, so they had to spend the night there before starting the hunt. Kamik remembered that his father had hit the bear in the leg. Maybe they would spot the blood on the snow and follow it, if the snow had not buried it. Tomorrow they would find out.

OORAMIK WAS NOT COMFORTABLE. She kept thinking about the hunters. She tried to work hard, but couldn't keep her mind off the danger they would face if they found the bear. She finally went out to her neighbour, Toogak.

'I will be staying with you until the hunters come back, Toogak. I am too restless alone. I hope you don't mind my staying with you?'

'I'll be glad to have you here, Ooramik. I feel lonely myself with my man away. You are very welcome.'

16

That night Soonah, the eldest man in the settlement, called a meeting of the entire people.

'I guess you all know why I call you to this meeting', Soonah said. 'As you all know, the bear came to our settlement to attack our dogs. I didn't want to bring up the subject of danger, and that's why it took me so long to call this meeting. But I realize we will have to face this danger. And it's time now. From his experience, Suluk thinks that this was a mad animal that struck our settlement. I am not saying this is true, but I am not saying he is wrong, either. We will have to be very careful from now on, and here is what I want everyone of you to do. Don't go out alone at night, and if you must go out, be sure to look around. Don't go far from the settlement during the day. And in case we are under attack, we must fight together. Anyone who spots a bear must send out an alarm. If attacked, we must fight the bear from all sides. And, most important of all, don't panic. I hope we don't have to fight any battle, but we must be prepared.'

THE BARKING OF DOGS woke the hunters up all of a sudden. Before anyone realized what was happening, the igloo came down on top of them. A great roar followed. Kamik knew what was happening. He had heard stories. This had happened too often. They were under attack by the bear.

Kamik had difficulty getting up from under the blocks of snow. He took his harpoon and started to turn toward the bear. He saw his father raise his arm, harpoon in

17

hand, but the bear made its move faster. It leaped toward
the lone figure. Kamik screamed a warning, too late. The
bear had its powerful jaws around Suluk's waist. Kamik
screamed and ran toward them. He could see the bear
shake its head, the body between its jaws. Kamik threw
his harpoon without thinking of aiming carefully, just
throwing it toward the bear. The harpoon struck. The
18 bear roared, dropped the still figure of Suluk, and leaped

for Kamik. While the bear was in midair, another harpoon struck its side. The harpoon came from Kisik's hand. Kamik fell with the bear on top of him. Before it could move, other hunters came and struck it from all sides, draining the life out. Kamik was helped from under the bear. As soon as he was free he ran to his father, who was lying in the snow, very still. With tears in his eyes, Kamik took his father on his knee.

Slowly Suluk opened his eyes, breathing very weakly. 'I am done for, Kamik. But for the sake of the others, get that bear. For the first time in my life, I feel there is a peace for me somewhere. At last I find peace. I shall rest forever in the peace which only dead people find. Someday you will find such peace, Kamik. I'll be waiting for you and for our people there.'

Kamik did not understand what his father meant about getting the bear. But then he realized that this was not the bear they were seeking. The bear they were after had a wound on its hind leg. This one hadn't. The hunt was not yet over. Now Kamik understood Suluk's words.

Next morning they buried Suluk on the island, and they covered the grave with the hide of the polar bear that had killed him. 'We will stay here the rest of the day and leave tomorrow', Kisik said. 'I made a silent promise to Suluk that I shall not stop until that bear is dead.'

But that night the sound of rising wind and snow told them that tomorrow would not be the day to travel; they would have to stay here until the blizzard was over. They couldn't go anywhere. Once in a while someone would go outside to relieve himself, and when he came back he was covered with snow and shaking with cold. For two   19 straight sunrises they couldn't go anyplace. On the third night the wind went calmer and calmer, and they knew this would be the day to start hunting again. At the first sign of dawn they began to make plans.

'We will travel for half of the day only, and use the other half to hunt for food for ourselves and our dogs', Kisik said. 'This way we will not tire our dogs so much and have a good chance to get food. And you all know how it feels to be hungry in this weather.'

'That reminds me', Kamik said. 'We have only enough meat for one more sunrise. When that meat is gone, what will we and the dogs eat?'

'Don't worry,' Kisik said, 'we have enough time to get seal. Or if we don't get seal in two sunrises from now, we have enough dead dog to eat and enough for our dogs too. I hope you have realized by now that after that blizzard some of our dogs are sure to be dead.'

Everyone went out to check on the dogs. Sure enough, two dogs had not survived the days of blizzard.

'But I have never eaten a dog in my whole life', Kamik said.

'This time you may have to, Kamik. It takes a lot of will power to survive', Kisik said sternly.

'You ever eat a dog?' Kamik asked.

'Yes.'

'How does it taste?'

'Terrible, just terrible!'

'That doesn't help much!'

'I know, Kamik. But maybe this time you will just have to taste one. I hope it won't be necessary. Now let's get ready to travel.'

THEY DIDN'T TRAVEL FAR THAT DAY. The snow was soft, which made things harder for the dogs; but though they were tired they kept going. That afternoon they made camp near a large ice ridge. This ice would act as a shield against the wind. After they had built an igloo, they went out hunting on a crack in the ice. They found three seal holes, and three of the hunters began to watch. For a long time they waited. Nothing came. The cold wind won, and they had to walk to keep warm. After the sun had set, they decided to destroy two holes and take turns on the one they did not destroy. Kisik was the first one to wait. But his feet couldn't take the cold and he had to quit. Immediately Naoolak took his place. Naoolak fought against the cold wind. His feet wanted to move, but he fought to keep still. Finally his mind began to go.

'Come on, you dumb animal', he whispered. 'You better come up. If you don't come up, I'll kill you!' At that moment he lost his temper. He broke his harpoon in half as he yelled and went down in the snow, beating his head against the ice and crying. Kamik, who was not far from him, realized what was happening. He began to run toward Naoolak. Then his heart jumped. He saw Naoolak getting up slowly. Naoolak took his harpoon, which was broken in half, and put the sharp point to his throat, ready to take his own life. Kamik jumped and got his hands on the harpoon. He tried to take it away from Naoolak's hands, but Naoolak, being older and stronger, threw Kamik down. Kamik was down, and he could see Naoolak above him, ready to throw the harpoon of death at him. Just as Naoolak threw, Kamik rolled to one side and the harpoon missed him by only a few inches. Kamik

21

got up and swung with all his might. His fist found its mark and Naoolak went down. At that moment the others arrived, got between them, and brought Naoolak back to his senses.

'Another dead man is not the answer to our problem', Kisik said toughly. 'If we are to survive and get the bear, we must think hard and straight. There will be no more violence, Naoolak. We have more of that than we care for, and I am sure there is more to come. But we must fight violence, not create it. Losing our tempers will help no one. Now control yourself.' Without saying anything, Naoolak walked away in shame. Now it was Kamik's turn to wait for the seal.

It was getting dark now and Kamik was getting cold, and as he waited he felt small in this dark world. He felt like crying. So many things had happened in a few sunrises—the mad bear, his father's death, dogs lost, and now this fight between him and Naoolak. He didn't blame Naoolak for what had happened. He didn't blame him for the way he had acted. Maybe all of them would act that way in time. But no! Nothing like that must ever happen again. To survive in this land they must be brave. The tears ran down his cheeks as he began to think about his mother. Suddenly he was brought back to the present by a bubbling sound from the seal hole.

Seal!

The seal was near. Kamik's heart pounded hard. He stopped breathing. Would the seal come up for air? He held his breath. An eternity later he heard a soft sound of breath from the seal hole. Wait! Wait for the right time. Don't strike too soon. Must strike at the right time.

22

Kamik aimed his harpoon directly at the seal hole and waited. Then he heard the heavy breathing of the seal. It suspected nothing. With all his might, Kamik struck.

A hit! Quickly he put his hands through the hole; the water was cold. He searched for seal. Was he strong enough to kill it? Was his aim true? Then he felt it. It was dead. He began to yell for help. The hunters came and wasted no time chopping the ice from the seal hole. Then they pulled the seal up. They began to jump and cheer and dance. For a few minutes there was no thought of all the things that had happened before.

'No dog meat for breakfast, dinner, supper!' Kamik cried as he danced.

That night they had a good meal, but they were careful not to eat more than was necessary. They had to save some meat to make it last as long as possible. Later, in bed, Kamik began to think of the bear again. Where will the bear strike next? Who will be the next victim? When will the people of the north, the Innuit, find rest?

Early next morning they set out again. Before the sun was up, they were travelling again, and all that day they travelled without seeing any sign of bear. Evening came and they made camp. They had hunted again without luck.

'We will not tie the dogs up this time', Kisik said. 'They will have more chance in case the bear attacks.' It was to be one of the deadliest mistakes.

Early next morning they began to get up slowly, one by one. They had a little meat for breakfast. Kamik was thankful this was not dog meat.

'It sounds like a nice day to travel', Naoolak said as he

23

was getting out. To his surprise, there were no dogs in sight. 'Hey! There are no dogs', he said as he quickly went back in.

'What do you mean?' Kamik asked.

'I don't see a single dog.' The same fear hit them all. They all went out quickly.

No dogs.

They saw dog tracks and followed them. Then they all stopped. In front of them were bear tracks. Fresh. Then they all knew why. The bear had come to their camp during the night. The dogs, being loose, had sighted the bear and gone after it.

'This is all we need!' Kisik said angrily.

'Do you think they will come back?'

' There is a chance they will come back, but that might take a day or two, or even a week.'

'What will we do next?'

'We will wait a day or two, and if they are not back by that time, we will start walking home.'

'Walk? But that is impossible. We are many sunrises away from home.'

'I know that, but it's all we can do. We can't wait here for long; the sooner we start the better. But we will wait here for one sunrise, and if they don't come by then, we start walking.'

'If we met a bear without dogs, we wouldn't have much power', Kamik said.

'There are eight of us, and we have harpoons', Kisik said. 'We have a chance.'

'Let's say there are seven and a half hunters', Kamik said. 'Remember, I am only half a hunter.'

'I wouldn't say that', Kisik said. 'Anyone who can kill a bear is a full hunter.'

Then Kamik remembered. His harpoon had struck the bear first the night his father was killed. According to the hunters' law, he had the right to claim the bear as his.

With all the provisions they could carry, they started walking toward home. They had waited for one sunrise, but no dogs had come. On the move, Kamik went to Kisik, who was leading the hunters.

'How long do you think it will take us to get home', he asked.

'Maybe ten sunrises, or maybe more—or less if we are lucky.'

'And what if we aren't lucky?'

'We won't get home.'

'Do you think we won't get home?'

'I can't say. It is a long way and there are dangers.'

'What will happen to our families if we don't get back?'

'I guess they will have to move to another settlement.'

'Think we have a chance to get home?'

'Yes, if we can go on without meeting any danger, and if we can kill some food on the way.'

With their harpoons in their hands, the hunters went on, armed only with their harpoons and their courage.

OORAMIK WAS TIRED. She hadn't slept well since the hunters left. She and Toogak had been living together and working together.   25

'Oh, those are beautiful boots you are making, Ooram-ik!'

'Thank you, Toogak.'

'I hope the hunters will be back soon', Ooramik went on. 'Our food is getting low again. I hope Mittik and Issa will get more seals.'

Issa and Mittik came back that night with three seals. Everyone cheered, and they all went to Mittik's house and had a feast.

TIRED AS THEY WERE, the hunters went on. Everyone of them was sweating, although the wind was cold. Kamik was the last in line. He stopped for a moment and wiped his face with snow. 'One thing for certain', he said to himself. 'If a man wants snow, there's plenty of it around.' For eternity they went on without resting. Finally their aching muscles couldn't take any more. Heavily they let their bodies drop, breathing hard. No one moved for a long time.

'How long to go yet?' Kamik finally broke the silence.

'Oh, maybe a hundred miles to go', Kisik answered.

'That's like a thousand miles, when a person has to walk.'

'I hope Issa and Mittik start to look for us soon', Naoo-lak said.

'I doubt if they will', Kisik said. 'Remember, they expect us to be gone for a long time. Besides, they have a whole settlement to look after.' They had a little meat to eat and once again started walking.

IT HAD BEEN SO LONG since the hunters had left that Oor-amik was sure something had happened. She decided to see Soonah and have a talk with him. She suggested to Soonah that they should hold another meeting. Soonah agreed, and everyone came to his house.

'I am sure I am not the only one with the feeling that something has happened to the hunters. They have been gone many sunrises now', Ooramik said. 'Nobody likes to think something has happened, but this is a wild land,

27

and anything *can* happen. Worrying and sitting won't help. We must do something.'

'But what can we do?' Soonah asked.

'There are two things we can do', Ooramik went on. 'First, Issa and Mittik can start looking. Second, they can go to the Kikitajoak people and ask for help.'

'But', Soonah said, 'between here and Kikitajoak there is a channel, and the ice is always moving. It never freezes all winter long. Anyone who tries to cross that channel has a chance of being carried out to sea.'

'I know all about that', Ooramik said. 'When I was just a girl, we crossed that channel. It can be done.'

'But we are still not sure the hunters are in danger, or that something has happened', Soonah argued.

'I think you are old enough to know that the hunters face danger every day, wherever they go. Lots of things can happen in only a few sunrises', Ooramik said. She went on, 'I think it's better that Issa and Mittik go to the Kikitajoak and ask for their help. They are only three sunrises away. With more men to search, they will have a better chance to find the hunters and to hunt for animal at the same time. Are you and Mittik willing to go?' she asked. They didn't answer. 'All right. If you won't go, I will. I'm taking your dogs and going to Kikitajoak myself. Who will go with me?'

'I will.' It was Toogak.

'No,' said Mittik, 'I won't let you do it. Two women wouldn't have a chance. I'm not giving you permission to take my dogs. It would be suicide for two women to try to cross that channel.'

'All right', Ooramik said, in tears. 'So we don't do any-

28

thing. But remember. If anything happens to those hunters, you will feel you were responsible for their death. Conscience will stay with you for the rest of your life.'

'All right,' Mittik said angrily, 'you can have the dogs. But remember, I won't be responsible for your death if you don't make it.'

'Just what makes you think we won't make it? We will make it, won't we, Toogak?'

'Are you right, Ooramik? I say you are right. We will make it.'

'Be ready at the first sign of dawn, Toogak.'

'I'll be ready.'

The two women went out, leaving the people speechless.

THEY LAY THERE MOTIONLESS, the only sound their breathing. With their faces in the snow, every muscle in their bodies refused to move. Kamik had gone to sleep where he dropped. He didn't care about the cold snow on his cheek. His aching muscles woke him up and he rolled over and stared at the stars. He wondered what the stars were made of, how they got there, why they shone at night when everything around was so dark. Then he saw northern lights. They were so pretty. How could this world have so many pretty things and yet be so cruel?

WAKE UP, TOOGAK, the daylight is almost upon us', Ooramik said as she shook Toogak violently. She was fully dressed and ready to go. 'I'm going over to Mittik now and tell him to get the dog team ready.'

She went out. Daylight was not far off, the wind was cold but calm. She went toward Mittik's igloo and suddenly sensed something was missing. She couldn't see any dogs. Had Mittik deceived her? She ran to his igloo, and just as she was coming in Soonah met her at the door.

'Where are the dogs? Where is Mittik?' she asked.

'Mittik and Issa are gone to Kikitajoak.'

'Why did they go?'

'I guess they felt ashamed the way they acted last night.'

'And I am sorry I acted so cruel last night', Ooramik apologized. 'I hope you will forgive me.'

'You are forgiven. I think you are a very brave woman, Ooramik.'

Then Ooramik went back to Toogak's igloo and found her still sleeping. There was nothing else she could do. She only hoped Mittik and Issa would succeed in their effort to reach Kikitajoak.

MITTIK AND ISSA WERE MAKING GOOD TIME. Their dogs were willing to travel and they were going faster than they hoped. Today they would have an easy trip, tomorrow would be a different story. There was a promise of danger when they crossed the channel. They might be carried out to sea, but there was no other way. Let danger come. They would fight it.

THE BIG ANIMAL TRAVELS SLOWLY, AIMLESSLY. His hind leg is in pain. He doesn't remember why his leg is in pain, his only thought is to get food. He cannot see clearly, his head is full of pain. He scents something ahead, maybe food. He goes to the top of an ice ridge to get a better view. He can see something white, and comes down from the ridge and walks toward it. Then he sees that it is another bear and it is eating something. He must get that food. He tries to run, but his leg is in too much pain. He roars to tell the other bear his intention. The other turns, ready to defend its food. They meet head on.

Their jaws open, slashing, biting. Sharp claws and powerful jaws find their mark. They go down together, and the snow becomes red with their warm blood. Their roar is like that of thunder. Their jaws find their mark once again. They taste each other's blood. Now one of them must be killed or run in defeat. They roll, bite, slash. It is all over. One roars a cry of victory over the motionless body of his victim.

The winner gets the food. He eats the dead seal. After a while he licks his wound. His wounded leg is in pain, he must rest. He wakes up again, much later, in great pain and hungry once more. There is no more food, he must hunt for food again. He gets up slowly and starts out for nowhere. His hind leg is in great pain, but still he must look for food. And darkness comes, and still no food. He is tired and hungry, but he must rest. He lies down. Here he will sleep without fear of being attacked. In this land he is king among animals. When he opens his eyes again, the darkness is gone, the pain is less, but still he is hungry. Today he must find food. He gets up slowly, he trav-

31

els slowly, not knowing where to go. Then he sees something ahead, small moving figures. The figures move toward him, but he decides to wait. Then he sees what they are, hunters on foot. Without dogs, the hunters will be easy prey. He must wait and surprise them.

THE HUNTERS TRAVELLED ON, not knowing that the eyes of danger were watching them. With their harpoons in their hands, they travelled for miles without stopping to rest. At last they all dropped to the ground, exhausted.

'Think there is a chance for us to survive?' Kamik asked the grandson of old Soonah.

'There is always a chance as long as we are alive', young Soonah answered. 'We have two chances—to make it on foot or to be found by the others if they decide to search for us.'

32

the Bear

CLOSE BY, THE BIG ANIMAL LIES WAITING for the right time to strike. That time will come; he must wait and be sure. Eight hunters can kill him, he must be careful. He wants to live and eight hunters will fill his empty stomach for many nights. Surprise is his best weapon. He must strike when they are at their weakest. He must not slip. Another few miles and he will have a chance to kill.

MILES WENT BY SLOWLY and the hunters were tired. Kamik was the last in line. He tripped on a chunk of ice and fell heavily on his face. He lay there for a minute trying to catch his breath, his lungs bursting. Then he sucked in the cold air and it felt good. He got up slowly. The rest of the hunters were out of sight. Slowly he started to walk again, taking his time. All of a sudden he heard a great roar and right away knew what it was. A bear.

Quickly he climbed to the top of a ridge to see. He stopped in horror. The bear was attacking the hunters. They had been caught off guard, not prepared for battle. Kamik saw the bear charging at full speed. The hunters threw their harpoons quickly, too quickly, not taking time to aim carefully. This mistake was to be their last. Only one harpoon struck the bear, on its shoulder, not enough to kill it. Kamik saw the bear lifting young Soonah in the air with its powerful front paw. Soonah screamed, hit the ground hard, and lay still. Quickly the bear was upon three other hunters, slashing and biting. They went down, never to get up again.

The remaining hunters drew their snow knives, small

33

weapons against such a big animal. Kamik knew that the hunters didn't have a chance. He wanted to rush out and fight beside them, but he knew that he wouldn't have a chance. It would be suicide to go there with half the hunters gone. Then the bear rushed the other hunters. Kamik knew that he couldn't face the bear alone and live. Then he remembered his father. His father had said that the bear must be killed at all cost. This was it. Kamik yelled as he got up from behind the ice and charged. The bear turned, dropping the still body of a man that he held in his mouth. The bear, too, was exhausted. He started toward Kamik slowly. Kamik held his ground, harpoon in hand. He dared not make the same mistake the others had made; he must hold onto his harpoon.

Kamik and the animal walked toward each other. They both knew only one of them would be alive when the battle was over. Kamik would fight to revenge his father's death and for the safety of the people; the bear would kill for food. Kamik knew that the next move was up to the bear. He dared not make the first move. If he threw the harpoon now, he was sure to hit the bear, but that wouldn't be enough to kill the beast. It takes more than one harpoon to kill a bear.

Then they met. Kamik had his harpoon between himself and the bear. The bear ran into it and the harpoon struck just under the throat. The bear roared and slashed. Kamik, now weaponless, dodged, got another harpoon from a dead hunter, and was ready once more. The bear, with two harpoons now in his body, was bloody. He charged again, but Kamik held his ground. The bear slashed, knocking the harpoon out of his hands.

34

Kamik ran to the harpoon lying in the snow, got it and turned, ready for more battle. Then his eyes opened wide in surprise. He saw Soonah trying to get to his feet; he was covered in blood. Soonah let out a cry, and the bear turned his attention and charged him. Kamik saw his chance. While the bear charged Soonah, Kamik

rushed him from behind. Just as the bear reached Soonah, Kamik thrust the harpoon into the beast's side. The bear roared in pain. Before he could turn, Kamik quickly pulled the harpoon out and struck again. The bear completed his turn and slashed, knocking Kamik off his feet. Now Kamik was at his mercy, without a harpoon. As the bear came for the kill, another shock came to Kamik. He saw Soonah get up with the harpoon and strike the bear

35

from behind. The bear went down. Kamik got up, took his harpoon, and struck the bear again and again. The bear roared its last.

Kamik went to Soonah and took him on his knee.

'I, too, made a silent promise, Kamik. It looks like we have kept our promise to your father. Tell my grandfather, Soonah, that I die happy. I'm going where there is everlasting peace.'

'I can't promise anything now, Soonah. I am the only one left, and no lone hunter can survive long in this land. Everyone is dead. Kisik, Naoolak, Napachee, they are all dead, and I expect to die soon.'

'Don't give up hope, Kamik. Remember what Kisik said before. There is always a chance. You must try.'

'Yes, I will go on, but I'm going to expect the worst.'

But Soonah didn't hear him. He was dead. Kamik had been given another chance to live by a half-dead man. For Soonah had been more dead than alive when he got up to help Kamik fight the bear. 'The people and the country will be saved as long as there are men like you in the land, Soonah', Kamik said. 'If I get out of this alive, I will try to be like you. I will do my part in taming this country.' For a long time Kamik held the lifeless body of Soonah. Soonah had found another peace, one that only dead people know about.

OORAMIK WAS TIRED AS EVENING CAME. She and Toogak were eating raw seal meat. As she chewed on the meat, she said, 'Why does life have to be so hard? Are we going

36

to struggle forever for survival? Sometimes I think I would be better off dead.' *Ooramik said*

'Don't say that, Ooramik. Who knows? Maybe things will change some day.'

'That is just a dream, Toogak.'

'But sometimes dreams come true.'

'Not in my life.'

FROM THE TOP OF THE ICE RIDGE, Mittik and Issa can see for miles around. Already the channel is visible far off on the horizon. They can see Kikitajoak across the channel. In that channel lies danger. All winter the ice floes move, floes that can carry a man out to sea if he doesn't travel quickly.

Before long they come to the edge of the channel. Now it is time to start. Issa keeps the dogs going with his whip while Mittik steers the sled. From here on they dare not stop for a single second. As they run and sweat, they can see broken ice crashing together, ice that can crush any living body if a man makes a wrong move. Luck runs out on them halfway across the channel. The dogs, too tired to run quickly, begin to make mistakes. One dog steps in the wrong place and goes under. It threatens to pull the rest of the dogs after it, so Issa has to cut the line. They never see a sign of that dog again. One dog lost, and they have only six more left.

' Let's just say we were lucky it wasn't one of us that went under', Mittik says. 'But we still have a long way to go.'

37

KAMIK BURIED THE BODIES OF HIS FRIENDS under the snow. They would be carried out to sea when the spring came, if a bear did not eat them first. It was not a pretty sight for a young man to see, all his friends bloody and lifeless; but he knew that somewhere their spirits were in peace. He turned and looked at the dead bear with hate in his eyes. Once again he remembered the torn bodies of his friends. Some of them had had their bellies opened by the sharp claws of the bear. Their organs showed. Naoolak's intestines were hanging out of his body. Kamik had vomited at the sight.

He went over to the bear. This was the bear that had killed so many hunters. Kamik was almost sorry it had died so quickly, without suffering. There was the old wound on its hind leg. This was the bear that was responsible for his father's death. He would have loved to have seen the bear dying slowly as young Soonah had died. Without another thought, Kamik took his snow knife and started to cut the bear.

WAKE UP, OORAMIK. You are having a nightmare', Toogak said as she shook Ooramik. Ooramik, shaking and crying, looked up at Toogak.

'I'm sorry, Toogak. I'll be all right now.'

'You were having a nightmare.'

'I dreamed of the hunters. I saw them dead in my dream. It looked so real.' *(Ooramik said)*

'I'm sure they're all right. You have just been thinking and worrying too much.'

38

'Why did they have to go?'

'You know why they had to go, Ooramik. They left so we can be better protected. So stop your worry and go back to sleep.' Although Toogak spoke these words, she wasn't sure the hunters were all right. 'I wonder how Issa and Mittik are making out?'

ALL THROUGH THE NIGHT they travelled on. With the darkness upon them, the danger had doubled. 'Another three hours or more and we will be out of danger', Mittik said.

'Yes, if we are lucky', Issa said, as he ran.

'Looks like we will have another cloudy day. I don't see any stars.'

'I hope we won't have any storm.'

'As soon as we get to the other side, even the storm won't stop us.'

'I've been saying to myself that we will make it, even if we have to crawl the rest of the way to get there.'

With hopes high, they went on through the night and its dangers.

KAMIK KNOWS THE STORM IS COMING. The wind is rising stronger every hour. The cold arctic wind blows in his face, but he doesn't care. He is hot and welcomes the cold wind. He can see the first sight of dawn. He has walked all night. If a storm does come, it will help him, for no wild animal travels when there is a storm. At least he will be safe from animals if a storm comes. By the time the sun is high, the snow is blowing and getting worse. Kamik shields his face with his hands to keep off the snow. With little hope for survival, he goes on. At least this time nature is on his side.

THE SOUND OF THE WIND beating against their igloo didn't help to ease Ooramik's mind. They hadn't said a word for an hour, but each knew what the other was thinking. Ooramik broke the silence. 'I hope the hunters will be back soon. If they aren't, we will be facing starvation.'

'I'm sure something good will turn up, Ooramik. I think you worry too much. Now, try not to worry.' But Toogak herself was worried. She knew that if the hunters, or if Mittik and Issa never came back they would face death by starvation.

AS THE WIND GOT STRONGER, the ice they were crossing on became more dangerous. The ice they were on moved and rocked violently. The dogs howled, and the salt water beat down on them and wet their faces, stinging their eyes. But thanks to their waterproof sealskin clothing the water didn't touch their bodies. The sound of ice crashing and the splashing of the water rang in their ears.

Each step they took would mean death if they stepped in the wrong place.

Some miles later they sighted safety. For the first time since they left the settlement, smiles showed on their faces. With happy smiles on their faces, they went on. Minutes later, they stepped onto the safety of solid, unmoving ice. They dropped to the ground; even the dogs went down. For the first time, they started to feel the aching muscles in their bodies. Issa tried to stand up and began to stagger and sway. Suddenly he fell flat on his back. He heard Mittik laugh.

'Don't try to stand up yet, Issa. Don't you know that we have been on the moving ice for so long that if we don't relax for a minute we will feel dizzy and fall.'

Later they got up and started once again in the direction of Kikitajoak and help.

THE STORM HAS GROWN WORSE, but Kamik goes on. He can see only a few steps ahead. Knowing wild animals will not travel in this storm makes him feel safe. But the wind itself is slowing him up, and he has to fight it hard each time he takes a step. He doesn't know just what is ahead, but he knows that if he keeps heading into the wind he is heading in the right direction. Sometimes he has to stop and wipe the snow off his face. The small store of meat on his back seems to weigh a hundred seals, but the meat is the most precious treasure he has now. Without food he won't survive another night. The snow is soft and makes travelling hard. He knows he must travel as far as possible each day if he is to make home. He wants to see his mother. This gives him the will to live.

THE TWO MEN WALKED BESIDE THEIR SLED, the dogs went slowly, the storm was upon them. But they didn't care. Kikitajoak was close; their only thought was to get there. 'There they are!' Both of them started to run, leaving the dogs to follow. At the settlement, a man who was feeding his dogs was the first to see them. Two men from the direction of the open channel! In a few minutes, there were hundreds of people outside. Some of the men started out to meet them. Issa and Mittik saw them coming and dropped to the ground to wait. From here on they wouldn't have to go for help. Let help come to them.

'What happened?' 'Who are you?' 'Where are you from?'

'We came here for help. You must help us. The hunters of our people are in danger.'

'All right. Come with us. You will tell us your story when you have eaten.'

Issa and Mittik had their first meal in three sunrises. After they had eaten, Issa told the story of the bear that had come to the settlement.

'A mad bear? Yes, that has happened before', one man said. 'A mad bear is dangerous. We must go, but not today.'

'And how is the channel?'

'Dangerous.'

'It's amazing how you made it across in this storm.'

'Yes, we were lucky. The storm didn't come until we were halfway across.'

'Your dogs will be fed. Your clothing will be dried. You must rest.'

KAMIK FALLS TO THE GROUND HEAVILY and doesn't bother to get up. His lungs are burning. The snow builds up around his body. He knows that if he stays like this he will be buried in a few minutes. He forces himself to get up. He knows that he has to make a small igloo to spend

43

the night in. He finds a good place to make one. A few minutes later he is struggling to put one block of snow on top of another. Each block seems heavier than the previous one. As he works slowly, the snow keeps falling on his face. It feels good, for he is sweating. After he has completed the igloo he goes inside. It is dark, but at least there is no wind. In darkness he chews a frozen piece of seal meat. It tastes good. After he has eaten, he spreads a small sealskin and lies down on it and tries to go to sleep.

He hears a noise calling him, 'Kamik, Kamik!' With a start he suddenly sits up. Then he realizes that it was only a dream. He has wakened in a cold sweat, the voice sounded so real. His heart beats faster and faster. Is the spirit of the dead trying to call him? There he lies, his eyes wide open in fear.

He doesn't know how he got back to sleep, but when he opens his eyes again the igloo is no longer dark. He gets up and goes outside. The wind is still blowing strong, but the storm has passed. He goes to the top of an ice ridge and looks all around. He can see the mountains far away, maybe three sunrises away. He decides he will head for those mountains, but once near them he must stay and travel on ice. He knows there is more danger on land than there is on sea. Wolves and musk oxen roam the land, living on anything they can kill. Wolves will not attack a man unless he is sleeping, but the musk ox is different. Kamik goes down from the top of the ridge and goes inside his igloo. He has a small piece of meat. Shortly he starts to walk again. He wonders. Will this be his last day? He isn't sure that he will stay alive long enough to see another sunrise.

44

Mittik didn't know how long he had slept, but when he opened his eyes he saw that everyone was up, and they were all eating. Without saying a word he started to get up. At this time Issa came in.

'Everyone is getting ready, Mittik. If you don't want to be left behind, you'd better hurry. Or would you rather stay in Kikitajoak where there are lots of women?' Issa asked, smiling.

'For that reason I would rather stay here, but I guess I'd better not', Mittik said. 'My woman would come after me with a harpoon in her hands. By the way, how many are coming back with us?'

'There will be twenty-one in all, with as many as a hundred and fifty dogs.'

'Why that's as many as our whole population at home, and I don't think we have that many dogs in our whole settlement', Mittik said.

At the first sign of the rising sun they were all ready. At a signal they all went toward the channel and its dangers. Mittik was surprised to see a girl among them. 'Now what would a girl be doing here on this trip?' he asked himself. They reached the channel not many hours later. With the wind calm the ice wasn't moving fast, but they knew that it still hid many dangers. One by one the teams jumped to moving ice. The dangerous crossing had started.

Tired as he is, Kamik doesn't dare rest. He knows each mile brings higher hope for survival. He is sweating, the little sack on his back seems to weigh a hundred seals. 45

The knife he is holding seems to try to force him to fall. Each time he takes a step, his feet refuse to move as quickly as he commands. His lungs are burning and his heart is beating like a sealskin drum. Still he forces every part of his body to move. While day is here, he must go on until his command is refused.

THEY WERE NOW IN THE MIDDLE OF THE CHANNEL. So far nothing had happened. But everyone knew there were still many dangers every step of the way. So far they had been lucky. How long would their luck hold? Angootik and his daughter Putooktee were leading the whole team, with Issa and Mittik right behind them. Issa smiled as he looked at Putooktee jumping expertly from one piece of ice to another. Then he looked behind. 'With this power we will find the hunters and the bear all right', he thought. 'People like this will control the wild country and its dangers.'

Tonight there would be no sleep for the people of Kikitajoak; they would have to travel all night. It would not be easy to travel in the darkness. While it was still daylight they had a chance to make the crossing without casualty, but they knew that they would have to cross at night as well and that darkness was not far. Soon danger would double.

46   DARKNESS COMES SLOWLY as Kamik moves on. He wants

to stop and rest, but he keeps saying to himself that he must move on while there is a little daylight. So far he has been lucky. Another day is almost past and he is still alive. Soon he will stop and make an igloo for the night.

When darkness comes he can go on no longer. He drops to the snow and rests. Slowly his body begins to relax. He doesn't want to get up again but forces himself to start looking around for a place to build a small igloo. He finds a good spot, and soon he is struggling to put one snow block upon another. It seems a long time later that he at last completes his construction. Once inside, he takes out a small piece of meat and chews on it hungrily. He can feel the cold frozen meat as it settles in his stomach. He forces himself to stop while there is a small piece of it left. This meat is his hope for survival before starving to death. By his side is his harpoon, which can mean life or death. The harpoon, which is so small, yet holds such power.

After he has put the small piece of meat in his sack, Kamik puts some snow in his mouth and melts it. When it has melted, he washes his hands with it and drinks what is left. He wipes his hands on his sealskin pants and lies down. He tries to close his eyes to sleep, but sleep will not come. Now he can do no more, only wait for tomorrow.

MANY HOURS LATER they sighted safety. They had been lucky that there had been no tragedy, with night upon them. Now here was safety, only a few steps away. One by one the teams got on solid ice. Wearily they stopped and dropped to the hard ice. From here nothing would stop them from getting to the settlement that Mittik and Issa came from. Here in safety they would stop and rest and eat. As soon as that was over they would go on. Putooktee was busy making a meal for the hunters when she heard someone approaching. In the darkness she saw the figure of a man. She asked, 'Who are you?'

'It's me, Issa. How are you?'

'Oh, I guess I'm a bit tired after that crossing.'

'That was no place for a woman', Issa said.

'I've gone through lots of danger. Who hasn't?'

'For a woman you did more than your share of helping', Issa said.

'Do you think we have a chance to find those hunters?' she asked.

'We'll find them all right. But the question is, will we find them dead or alive?'

'You don't think they're dead, do you?'

'In this land you have to expect the worst', Issa said.

'I know, but it's not a nice thought', she said. Then, 'Do you have any relatives on that party?'

'My brother Naoolak is with them, and my friend Kamik, who is only sixteen winters and summers old, is also with them. I know all of them, and they are good hunters', Issa said. 'Now let's hear about you.'

'Well, there's not much to tell', she began. 'My name is Putooktee, as you know. My father is Angootik; he is the leader of the people of Kikitajoak. My mother died when I was very young. I have one brother and one sister, and I am the youngest of the family. When I was young I was

48

restless, more interested in man's work than woman's. I guess that's why I took to travelling with my father. I have learned a lot about man and his job. I guess I will always be a wanderer, never wanting to stay in one place very long, always hungry for action and adventure.'

'Don't you think about marriage?' Issa asked.

'No, at least not yet. I am uncertain about that', she said.

'You are very pretty. If I weren't married now, I would ask your father for your hand in marriage', Issa said.

'If Netsiak heard you say that, he wouldn't like it', she said.

'Who is he?'

'He is a man who is with us on this trip, a very jealous man who has a quick temper. He has tried to marry me before, but my father refused him. I'm glad he did. I don't like Netsiak.'

'I'll be very careful from now on. I don't want to start trouble', Issa said, smiling.

'I guess I'd better call the hunters that the meal is ready.'

At the sound of Putooktee's call, everyone dropped their work and started eating hungrily. This was their first meal since they started the trip. Issa took his meat and sat on a large piece of ice. A heavy-built man with a large piece of meat in his hands sat next to him.

'Hello', Issa said.

'I saw you talking to my Putooktee a while ago', the big man said as he chewed on the meat hungrily.

'Oh, I didn't know she was married', Issa said calmly.

'She's not married to me yet, but she will be married to

49

me someday', Netsiak said.

'Oh, that's nice. When did her father say you can marry her?' Issa asked.

'Her father hasn't said anything yet, but he will', Netsiak said. 'And one more thing, stranger. You stay away from my Putooktee if you don't want trouble with me.'

'Now just a minute', Issa said, staring directly into Netsiak's eyes. 'You said you weren't married to her yet, so why all this "My Putooktee" talk? She is not yours yet, and I can talk to her any time I want to. You speak harsh words, but I'd like to see you face a bear and see how big a man you are', Issa said.

Netsiak's eyes hardened as he said, 'Just a warning, stranger. If you don't stay away from her, you will feel

the tip of my harpoon in your throat.'

'Thanks for the warning. I'm not looking for trouble, but I'll be waiting for your move with the harpoon in my hands. And to be fair, I'll tell you this. Anyone has a right to talk to anyone', Issa said.

'Not to my Putooktee', Netsiak said harshly.

'You're wrong', Issa said calmly. 'You can't take anyone's freedom with your tough talk. You don't scare me at all.'

'You just wait', Netsiak said.

'Goodbye, animal, I will see you again', Issa said, smiling as he walked away.

All through the night they travelled. They would reach the settlement before the sun was high. Then the real hunt would begin.

ANOTHER DAY COMES FOR KAMIK. Once again he is ready. His muscles are sore from the previous day, but he tries not to think about it. No matter where the pain comes from, he must fight it; this is the only way to reach home. There is a strong wind blowing, but still he is hot as he walks. He wishes he was cold instead, for when a man is cold he can walk faster and easier. He rubs some snow on his face and it immediately melts against his warm cheek. Much later he comes to the rough ice. This will make it much tougher than smooth ice, and it will tear his caribou skin boots more quickly. Still he must go through it, to go around would waste many hours. He knows that before he reaches home he will be almost barefoot, his

51

boots will be spent. With the soles gone he will be exposed to the snow, and frostbite will come. He knows how it feels to have frostbitten feet. But there are many things to worry about before that time comes. He knows he can run into trouble any minute from now.

I AM GOING TO GET SOME ICE for water, Toogak', said Ooramik.

'Please be careful, Ooramik. Remember what old Soonah said to us.'

'Yes, I'll remember his words. Don't worry, I will look around.' Ooramik went outside and looked. She opened her eyes wide.

'They're coming! They're coming!' she yelled, as she went back to Toogak.

'Who? Who?' asked Toogak as she struggled to put on her boots.

'The people of Kikitajoak!' Ooramik spread the word, and soon everyone was out to greet Issa and Mittik and the people of Kikitajoak. The wives of Issa and Mittik ran to their husbands with tears of joy. Everyone greeted one another, and soon all the people of the settlement went to the meeting.

'My name is Angootik, and I am leader of this party', Angootik said. 'Since it's too late to go anywhere tonight, we will have to spend a night here. However, we will start out tomorrow at the first sign of dawn. I will be asking you for information about the hunters, and I hope you will be able to give it, for the information I'm going to ask is vital and we need to know where to start. How long have they been gone now?'

'Seventeen sunrises', Soonah answered.

'And how much food did they take?' Angootik asked him.

Soonah answered, 'Enough to last them five or six days.'

'Five or six days, hunh? I'm sure if they haven't caught any animals they must be hungry by now, so we'll take lots of seal and caribou and fish meat', Angootik said. 'And what direction did they take?'

'Toward Aivik Island.'

'Did they say how long they were planning to stay?'

'Until they find and kill the bear.'

'All right. This could mean they are still looking and are perfectly all right; or it could mean that they have lost so many dogs due to starvation that they are slow in travelling. Or they could be here any time now', Angootik said. He went on, 'And can anyone tell me how this bear they were seeking acted?'

Soonah answered, 'This bear was mad all right. No ordinary bear would attack the dogs so violently without eating them. And no normal bear would come right into the settlement just to fight the dogs.'

'I hope I am wrong,' Angootik said, 'but from what you describe I think this bear has rabies. If this is true, it is a very dangerous animal.'

'How does an animal get rabies?'

'I really don't know how it starts,' Angootik said, 'but lots of animals, especially foxes, are affected—and dogs too. And I know from experience that when a person gets bitten by a rabid animal he will die within a few sunrises. So I hope there are no dogs that are affected in this settlement now.' Angootik went on, 'Anyone who wishes to go with us is welcome to do so. I know you are anxious to see your relatives as soon as possible.'

'I wish to go', Ooramik said. 'My husband and my son are in that party.'

'And I', Toogak said. 'I'm tired of sleeping alone. I need my husband very much, especially at night.' Everyone laughed.

'All right. We will start out at the first sign of dawn', Angootik said.

KAMIK HAS TRAVELLED FAR. The ice he is walking on is rough, and already he can see that the soles of his boots are beginning to tear. He can see the mountains clearly now, but they are still maybe two sunrises away. And he only hopes he will not see bear on the way. He is hungry, but he doesn't dare eat what he has left. The meat he is carrying is too small. He plans to eat it at sunset time. He doesn't dare stop and look for seal holes. This would take too much time. His feet feel pain as he steps on a sharp piece of ice, but at least they are warm. He knows that as soon as he stops walking he will feel cold. He feels so tired and so hungry that he almost wishes he were dead. But no, he mustn't talk or think like that. He is suffering to live. Death comes easy, and he must fight to live. He has lived through many deaths and walked away; he must reach home. He is so deep in thought that he

54

doesn't try to get up, but lies with tears rolling down his cheeks. For a long time he doesn't move. He looks at his harpoon lying a few steps from him. He takes it in his hands and stares at it for a long time. Kneeling in the snow, he slowly puts the sharp tip of the harpoon to his throat. One move and he will suffer no more. Quickly he throws it down and once again falls to the snow, crying loudly.

A long time later he sits up, staring sightlessly at the sky. 'Taking my own life will not change things', he says to himself. 'A good hunter does not give up easily. I must control my madness.' He thinks how his mother would feel. And once again he falls down and cries.

Night comes and he can no longer go on. He is starting to build his igloo when a thought strikes him. Maybe he has a better chance travelling by night than by day. Surely if he can't see the animals because of darkness, then animals can't see him either. One thing, though. Animals smell without seeing, and he doesn't. He will have to take chances. Travelling by night is a good idea, but he will have to sleep very little. He decides he must take the chance. He stops cutting snow, takes out his meat, and chews on it. This is the last meat. He eats all of it. Now he is facing death by starvation as well. He must plan.

He decides he must hunt. This will slow him, but he has no choice. Without food he will starve. He must hunt during the day and sleep little. If he gets food, he will continue toward home at night. He decides to hunt near land when he gets there. If he doesn't get food from the sea, he will hunt on land for musk ox, wolves, ptarmigans—anything, even lemmings. He will hunt near those mountains. If he fails to get food, he will choose to die there. With this plan in mind, he walks on into the night.

THE SOUND OF HOWLING DOGS broke the silence in the small settlement. The dogs sensed that the time had come to travel again. One by one, figures appeared out of small igloos. The people were getting ready while it was still dark. Out on the horizon the first sign of dawn appeared, and the people saw a promise of a good, clear, sunny day. There was no sign of cloud. The sun was lighting half the sky to the east when the people left the settlement. Ooramik was with Angootik and Putooktee. Toogak rode with Issa and Mittik. It was decided that Issa and Mittik were needed on this trip; they knew the land and would act as guides. Two men from Kikitajoak took their place to look after the people remaining at the settlement.

Their first destination was Aivik Island; that was the place to start looking for hunters. In the sled, Ooramik sat sadly. No words were spoken, only the patter of feet and the crackling sound of sleds could be heard. From Aivik Island their destination was unknown. They had a hope of sighting sled and dog tracks. If they did sight them, they would follow them until they found the hunters. It was a bright day, the sun shone down upon them, it was warm, they could see for miles. They travelled all day with few stops to rest and eat. They had no hope of finding a sign of hunters this day, but tomorrow could tell a different story.

All that day they travelled on, and far into the night. When they could no longer see far, they made camp in the middle of nowhere. The day had ended and tomorrow was waiting. Six igloos were built to spend the night in. After feeding their dogs, they went to their igloos and ate frozen meat of caribou, fish, and ptarmigan. Ooramik and Toogak stayed with Angootik and Putooktee. They ate quietly. Then Ooramik asked, 'How long do you think, before we find them?'

Angootik said, 'It may take many sunrises, or it could be tomorrow. It's hard to say. But we will find them no matter how long it takes.'

'But if you are gone for so long, won't your family and your people miss you and go hungry?'

Angootik answered, 'There are many people and much meat in Kikitajoak. They will not go hungry. As for myself and my family, there is no one in Kikitajoak who

will miss me and Putooktee. My other children are all married and have their own problems.' He went on, 'I keep wondering why you people choose to stay in this land, why you don't move to Kikitajoak where there is much animal to feed many people.'

Ooramik said, 'Everyone is scared to try to cross the channel that never freezes. Too many lives of women and children would be risked.'

'I see', Angootik said. 'But if people are interested in moving to Kikitajoak, this will be their chance. After finding the hunters, we can talk this over and see if they want to move.'

Once again silence followed. One by one they lay down on their caribou skin beds and tried to sleep.

WHEN KAMIK OPENS HIS EYES it is dark. He has slept too long and night has come. His little caribou skin offers small protection from the cold night air. He rises slowly and stretches; his muscles are sore. But he must start again. Another night and he is sure he will reach the mountains. That will be the place to start hunting for food.

The lone figure moves slowly. He travels in darkness, never sure what lies ahead. The snow he is walking on is hard and hurts his feet. His feet are beginning to feel cold, the soles of his boots are torn. Even in darkness he can see the mountains ahead. Today he must get food or he will grow weak from hunger; and he knows he must be strong to survive. He decides he will hunt before going to sleep again. He will hunt in the daytime and sleep at night. He is thankful that this is the last night in which he will have to travel. Once at his destination, he will hunt until he gets food or until starvation comes.

He is exhausted by the time first daylight appears on the horizon. He has walked all night without rest, but his endless walk has been rewarded. Now his destination is close. From here on he will look for seal holes. Much later, he finds a good seal hole. He waits until his feet can't stand the feel of cold snow. He has to stop watching and walk for a while. When his feet get warmer, he goes back to the seal hole again and waits. Now darkness comes close again, and still no food. He is weak now. No food and too much travel have begun to take their toll. He can feel the first signs of starvation. Darkness comes and he begins to build an igloo. This will be his home until he gets food and can go on, or until death comes. When he has completed his igloo, he sits inside. It is dark and cold. The only possessions he has now are his harpoon, his ivory knife, a sealskin rope, his sealskin sack.

A sealskin sack!

A sealskin sack is food. He has been carrying food all along and didn't know it. His sack is dry, but it is food. 'He told me once that when you're facing starvation anything made of animal can be eaten', he thinks, remembering his father's words. 'My sack, my rope, my clothes and caribou hide are all food.' He takes his knife and picks up his rope. Tonight he will eat it. Tomorrow he can eat what's left of it. When that is gone he will start on his sack. This will give him a hope of surviving until he can kill an animal. He chews on the rope wildly. It is

59

tasteless, still it is food. It makes him feel better in the stomach.

Still more surprises.

His sack and caribou hide! He can tear his caribou hide and make himself soles for his boots. He will use the rope and wrap the hide around his feet. With these thoughts, he smiles. The clothing he wears will be his food as well. With better hope he lies down, and sleep comes instantly.

Hopes give him strength

With the sun shining brightly in a cloudless sky, Kamik comes out of his small igloo. He looks around. The wind is calm; this will be a good day to hunt for seals. He goes back inside and takes his sealskin rope. He takes his knife and cuts the rope into small pieces. This done, he chews on the rope hungrily. After he has eaten, he goes out again with his harpoon and his knife in his hands. He looks up to the great cliff. It is high, like trying to reach heaven. The cliff is straight up. To get to the top, he will have to go around to the other side. But that will be another day. Today he will hunt seals in the sea. If he fails to get food, he will hunt on the land next. Some time later he finds a seal hole. It is good, and his hopes are now higher. He begins his first wait. He must be patient; he knows that in everyone's life patience is important.

Darkness comes again. Kamik has waited all day and no seal has come. He is tired and hungry. He knows that tonight he will have to eat sealskin rope again. He decides that tomorrow he will hunt on the land. He is weak and he starts back toward his small igloo.

The first ray of the sun is hitting the sky as Kamik goes out. He is hungry and cold, but at least he has had a good night's sleep. He starts toward the mountain, to its right side. He can see that the cliff is lower on that side. He knows that it will take a lot of strength, something he doesn't have now, but he has no choice but to climb. The land is his last hope. The edge of the cliff is rocky and it hurts his feet. Still he struggles. He looks down to where he was at sunrise. He is high, and he knows that if he slips he will roll and never stop until he gets to the bottom. He knows he will die before reaching the bottom.

The sun is high by the time he gets to the top. He is sweating and out of breath; he lies still for a long time. Wiping the sweat from his face, he feels better. As he gets slowly to his feet, he gets a shock. The howling sound of wolves—and close. Holding his harpoon tightly in his hands, he goes toward a rock. When he reaches the rock he looks over it and his eyes open wide. He sees three wolves attacking four musk oxen, the wolves howling as they start toward the musk oxen, which have formed a circle to protect their young one. One bull gets out of the circle and charges at one wolf. The wolf dodges and the musk ox misses its mark. Kamik knows musk oxen are helpless against such foes. He knows wolves don't fear animals. They fear man.

'They fear a man', Kamik thinks. He looks back where he has just come from. Then a thought strikes him. It is dangerous, but then again he has been in danger for so long that it makes no difference. He suddenly exposes himself to the wolves and musk oxen. With a yell, and waving his arms wildly, he goes toward the beasts. The wolves stop their attack and look at him. Seeing the man, the wolves leap and are off. The musk oxen stay in their circle unmoving. Now it is time to proceed to his plan. Yelling loudly, Kamik goes toward the circle of musk oxen. He knows that sooner or later the bull will charge him. This is part of his plan. Now he is close enough to hurl his harpoon. He knows that one strike will never kill a musk ox, but with all his might he hurls the harpoon. It goes straight and fast toward the bull. The harpoon strikes the beast on its side. Now Kamik is sure the bull will charge. The big beast jumps and charges at Kamik. Kamik runs toward the cliff with the beast a few steps away.

Will his plan work, or will the bull get to him before he reaches the edge of the cliff?

Kamik gets to the edge and turns. He sees the beast charging at him at full speed. When the bull is only a few steps away, Kamik steps aside and lies flat on the snow. The bull, with the harpoon in its side, doesn't stop. Too late, the beast sees the cliff and tries to stop, but it is going too fast. It falls over the cliff to certain death. Kamik's plan has worked. Now all he has to do is climb down to the dead animal and eat. Climbing down is not easy, with every chance to slide down and die. But with food waiting at the bottom, Kamik goes down without thinking of danger. At the bottom, he finds the dead animal. At once he starts cutting. After he has cut the animal, he eats wildly and licks at its blood. It is good. Now he has every chance to get food, and takes all he can eat. Now he has food for many sunrises. Maybe he will get home after all.

He gets back to his igloo at sunset. He carries a heavy load of meat on his back. After he has put all the meat away, he lies down. He feels sick. He knows why he is sick. After too many days without food, he has eaten too much. He hopes the sickness will be gone by morning.

musk oxen

HERE ARE SOME TRACKS', Angootik said, as he pointed at the tracks of dogs and sleds. Everyone came and looked. 'They went through here', Angootik said. 'Now we will find them.' They all went toward where the tracks led. All that day they followed the tracks. At dusk they found signs of tragedy.

'Here is where they slept', Angootik said. 'And look!' He pointed at the ground. 'Blood and bear tracks, indicating that they met the bear.'

'Look,' someone yelled, 'here are more tracks leading to the top of the island.'

'What do you suppose they went up there for?' Mittik asked Angootik.

'There's only one way to find out', Angootik said. 'Let's follow them.'

They followed the tracks and, once on top, they all knew what they were looking at. A grave.

Ooramik ran to the grave, and fell on top of the grave, and cried, not controlling her crying. Issa took her gently by the arm and took her away from the grave.

'We must uncover the grave and see who it is', Angootik said. While they uncovered the grave, Issa held Ooramik closely. The dead man was exposed. Mittik knew who it was. He turned to Ooramik. 'It's Suluk', he said.

Ooramik tried to free herself from the hands of Issa, who was holding her closely. 'It's better you don't see him', Issa said to Ooramik. 'If you see him like this, the memory will always haunt you.'

After covering the body, they left the grave and got back to their sleds. There they spent the night. All the next day they followed the tracks, and by sunset they

64

found another igloo where the hunters had spent the night.

'We're on the right track, all right', Angootik said. 'It's just a matter of time before we find them.'

Someone yelled, 'Here's more bear tracks!'

'And here are dog tracks. They went after the bear, by the looks of them', Issa said.

'But I don't see any sled tracks', Angootik said. 'This could mean the dogs went after the bear without pulling any sleds. This doesn't make sense.'

'Hey! Over here, everybody', someone yelled. 'Here are some man tracks.'

'The hunters' tracks,' Angootik said, 'travelling in the opposite direction from the dogs and bear. Something is not right.' They followed the tracks for a while on foot.

'I hope I am wrong,' Angootik said, 'but from here it looks like the hunters lost their dogs and are travelling home on foot.'

'I think you're right', Mittik said. 'Everything indicates they left here some time ago on foot, when the dogs left and went after the bear.'

Angootik said, 'Since they could be travelling on foot, they can't be far. This means we could catch up with them soon.' They went back to their dogs and made a plan.

'We're not sure yet,' Angootik began loudly, 'but we think the hunters are travelling home without dogs; and without dogs their power against any enemy, such as bear or distance, is greatly reduced. We must find them quickly, before they run into any bear.' He paused for a moment and went on. 'And I guess you all know that a

65

man is very weak against a bear, without dogs on his side. So we must not rest until we find these hunters.'

Without hesitation they left. All through the night they went on. Some men had to follow the tracks on foot, ahead of the dogs. Sometimes they lost the tracks and had to turn back to start another trail. Next day they found another sign of tragedy. The dogs sniffed, and with a howl they jumped and followed the scent. The people knew something was ahead. The dogs stopped and sniffed, and dug at the snow. The people looked around and saw blood all over the snow. The dogs began to sniff and dig. One dog exposed a human leg. Issa was the first to see the leg.

'Oh no!' he said. Everyone looked. What they saw was not pretty. A human leg. Toogak fainted at the sight.

'All right,' Angootik said, 'everybody move back. Two of you dig up there and see whose body it is.' He went to Issa and said, 'I'm sorry, but I'm going to have to ask you to identify the dead man.'

Three men dug the snow and, to their horror, more bodies were found in the same hole. A moment later the bodies of the hunters were dug up and identified by Issa. 'Only one unaccounted for', he said to Angootik.

'And who's that?' Angootik asked.

'Young Kamik is not among the dead', Issa answered. 'That could mean he is still alive or he is lying dead somewhere else.' Then they found the bear skin.

'It's all clear now', Angootik said. 'They killed the bear here, but at the cost of these hunters. It looks like only one is still alive.'

66   'Or was alive', Mittik said.

'Yes', Angootik said. 'I was told Kamik is not among the dead. This means he has buried these hunters. And, since they killed the bear, that means he was not killed. Our next problem is to find him if he is still alive.'

'Where can we begin?' Mittik asked.

Angootik answered, 'At this stage, Kamik's only choice would be to get home the shortest and quickest way. So we must look for his tracks in a direction toward home.'

Ooramik came in tears and said, 'Please find him. We've got to find him. He's all I have left. Don't let him die now.'

Angootik said, 'We will do all we can. And please don't feel you are left without a friend. We are all brothers and one family.' Then he turned to all the people and said, 'First of all we will have to find Kamik's tracks. It will be difficult since this is a place of rough ice. We must travel separately and hope one of us will find his tracks. And we must look carefully on all clear ice, since tracks are easy to find there and will not be buried even during a storm once they are in clear, smooth ice.'

Before they left, they sank the bodies of the hunters in a crack. After they had done that, they went on in groups of two to search for signs of tracks. It was decided that if they found any sign one of the pair would notify the rest while the other stayed where he had found the tracks. Darkness came, and the searchers were forced to stop and spend the night separately. When dawn came, they continued the search without finding any sign. It was late in the afternoon when Neklik and Ashoonak found the tracks in a small clearing. 'He went through here', Neklik said. 'You must find the rest and tell them of our finding.' Ashoonak went, leaving Neklik at the tracks.

By sunset everyone had come to the tracks, and moments later everyone was on the right trail again. 'We will have to camp here', Angootik told everyone.

Ooramik went to Angootik and said, 'But can't we go farther?'

'No, Ooramik', Angootik answered. 'I realize how anxious you are to find your son, but we can't afford to lose his trail again, and in darkness we are sure to lose it. I'm sorry, but we must wait until dawn comes.'

'You think we will find him?'

'We will find him all right,' Angootik said, 'but the question is, will we find him alive or dead?' Ooramik sank down and cried. 'But don't worry', Angootik went on. 'Everything indicates he got this far alive, and we have every hope to find him alive.'

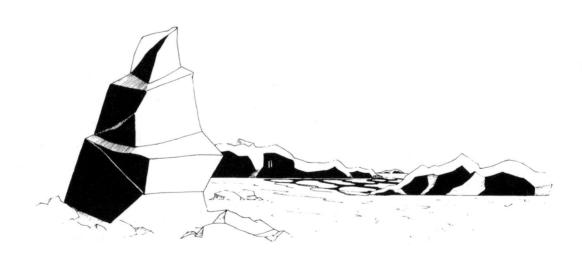

Angootik turned away and said to himself quietly, 'Don't let me fail now. Great Spirit, help me! Guide me! Where is the boy?'

KAMIK HAS TRAVELLED ALL DAY without rest. He hasn't got far, but he has gained another day without danger, and he is tired as he lies in his small igloo. It has been a hard day, maybe harder than any other day he has travelled. The meat he carried was heavy. It was hot, without wind. The night has come too soon for him. He is tired and needs rest, but he had wanted to get farther than he is now. The longer he travels the closer he will get to home. For a long time, sleep doesn't come. He keeps listening for a sound. 'The sound of what?' he asks himself. Maybe he is listening for the sound of dogs and people, or maybe for the sound of the steps of a bear. The thought of a bear coming scares him. For a long time sleep doesn't come, and when he finally goes to sleep he begins to relive in his dream the day his friend was killed. In his dream he sees himself and young Soonah battling the bear. Suddenly he wakes up with a scream. He is sweating. Then he realizes it is only a dream. He listens for a sound and none comes. He lies with fear in his eyes, and sleep will not come.

DAYLIGHT CAME AND THE PEOPLE OF KIKITAJOAK were once again ready. Men were ordered by Angootik to run ahead

69

of the dog teams and follow the tracks of Kamik.

'It looks to me as if he were heading for those mountains over there', Angootik said. 'I think I'm going to have to change my plans.' Angootik told everyone to stop and listen to his next plan.

With everyone gathered around him, he said, 'We are doing this the right way, but we are going far too slow. I want half of you to follow on as you have done, making sure you don't lose those tracks; and I want half of you to follow me to those mountains.' He pointed. Then he went on, 'By the looks of his tracks, it seems that Kamik was heading for those mountains. We are going on, but some of you stick with those tracks. If we don't find any sign of his tracks, we will come back to you; but if we find his tracks we will send someone to notify you.'

Then Angootik and half the party went ahead of the others. It took a long time to get to the mountains, but when they got there they found another sign. Once again the sharp-smelling noses of their dogs were their main help. The dogs howled, and sniffed, and started running. They stopped and fought over the bones. The people ran to the scene and stopped in surprise. They all stared at the musk ox skin and bones. Angootik was the first to speak.

'Here is another sign of how Kamik fights to survive', he said. 'It's all clear. He has been here and he has killed himself a musk ox.' He went on, 'We can tell from the crushed bones that the musk ox fell off the cliff. No doubt Kamik planned this. Now we know he is not starving and may still be alive.'

'From the looks of the tracks,' Issa said, 'Kamik was

here not long ago, and since he has to travel on foot he can't be far.'

Ooramik said, 'But night will be here again soon.'

Angootik said, 'I'm not going to disappoint you again, Ooramik. We are travelling all night. Since Kamik's tracks are not old, I'm sure our dogs can follow them by scent alone. And even if we lose them in the night, we will know where to start again.'

With brighter spirit they went on to follow Kamik's tracks. Right through the night they went on, depending on the dogs to follow for them. The way the dogs sniffed, Angootik knew the dogs were following a scent. Then they found a small igloo.

'Kamik spent a night here', Angootik said. 'Let's go on. We are on the right trail.'

Sunrise came and they were still on trail. 'From the look of those tracks, we can't be more than a day behind Kamik', Angootik said. 'I think we will find him alive.'

THE LOAD HE IS CARRYING forces Kamik to stop and rest. He takes the load off his back and sits on the ice. Just as he starts to lie on his back, he hears a roar. Kamik jumps to his feet and turns. He sees a bear. He takes his harpoon and runs to the top of a large ice ridge. Here, he decides, he will make his stand to the end. Kamik is surprised that the bear does not go after him. Instead it goes to his meat and eats it hungrily. Kamik watches the bear with fear. He knows that as soon as it has eaten his meat it will go after him. The great animal finishes the meat quickly and then turns to look at Kamik. Kamik knows this is the moment. The bear walks slowly towards Kamik and stops. He knows the bear is sure it will have another meal soon and is taking its time attacking the hunter. Kamik waits, holding the harpoon tightly, as the bear starts again slowly toward him. He holds his harpoon tightly between himself and the bear. He is high enough so that the bear will have to stand on its hind legs to touch him.

The bear roars and charges at full speed. Once reaching Kamik, it takes a slash at him with its powerful paw. Kamik holds his ground and the bear strikes the sharp end of his harpoon. Its leg cut and in pain, the bear roars in pain and goes to the ground. Kamik can see the blood, but he knows that a single cut like that will never kill the bear. The bear gets on its hind legs again and tries to jump at Kamik. Kamik holds his harpoon, and the bear

runs into it, and the harpoon cuts the bear on its shoulder. The blood comes.

Kamik grows tired and hot. His head throbs and his muscles are sore. He knows the bear can tire him out if he doesn't kill it fast. But killing a bear fast is impossible with only one harpoon. The bear comes at Kamik blindly and the harpoon cuts its forehead. Kamik sees blood all over, and hope comes. He thinks maybe if he is lucky he will kill the bear in time. Once again the bear charges at full speed. Kamik braces himself and holds the harpoon tightly. The bear jumps, and Kamik thrusts the harpoon toward the bear's neck without letting it go. The harpoon finds its mark and goes deep inside the bear's neck. Not wanting to lose his harpoon, Kamik holds onto it. The bear turns and hits Kamik on his side. Kamik goes flying down. He lands on his back heavily. He gets up in time to see the bear turn toward him. Now he is defenceless.

He sees the bear with his harpoon stuck in its neck. Then he thinks of his knife. He runs toward his knife which he had left beside the meat the bear had eaten. Not daring to look back, he dives for the knife. He gets it in his hand and turns. He sees the bear coming toward him slowly. Now on the ground, and with only a knife in his hands, Kamik knows the end has come. The bear comes slowly. Kamik steps back with hands spread wide, bracing for the fight to the last breath.

Suddenly many sounds come.

Kamik and the bear turn toward the noise at the same time. They both see dogs and men, coming fast. Men with harpoons and the dogs growling. Kamik has been found.

THE BEAR SAW ITS HOPE DIE. It turned and tried to run away from the dogs and harpoons, too late. The dogs came in hundreds, biting, howling. Right behind the dogs came men with expert knowledge of how to kill. The harpoons flew and struck. The bear went down.

Kamik fell to the ground breathless. He looked up and saw his mother. Ooramik ran toward him with tears of joy. Kamik got up and received his mother. For a long time they held each other with tears of happiness. For a long time no one spoke. Kamik finally let go of his mother and looked around. He saw many strangers, but among them he recognized Issa, Mittik, Toogak.

'These are all people of Kikitajoak', Ooramik said. 'Issa and Mittik went to Kikitajoak and summoned them to help us.'

'Thank you', Kamik said. 'I owe all of you my life.'

Angootik came forward and said, 'My name is Angootik. I am leader of Kikitajoak. This is my daughter, Putooktee. We are happy to see you alive. You are a very brave man.'

'And very lucky', Kamik said. 'I wish I could say the same about the others. You saw what happened to the others, didn't you?'

'Yes', Angootik said. 'I am very sorry we came too late to help the others.'

'You must be hungry and tired, Kamik', Ooramik said. 'Come, we will feed you.'

'And we will spend the night here', Angootik said. 'We must rest our dogs and wait for the others. I guess Ashoonak won't mind finding the others and telling them we are here.' Right away Ashoonak left.

THAT NIGHT KAMIK TOLD EVERYONE what had happened during the entire trip. He fought back the tears as he told how his father had lost his life, and how they were attacked by the bear and he alone survived and saw his friends' torn bodies, and how he had fought to survive the blizzard and starvation. He looked at his mother and Putooktee and Toogak, and they were all in tears.

'I am sorry about the tragedy that has come,' Angootik said, 'but now you must think of the future.'

Ooramik said, 'Angootik has suggested that we move to Kikitajoak. What do you think, Kamik?'

'I don't know yet', Kamik answered. 'The decision is up to the people and you, Mother.' Without saying another word, Kamik went out. Ooramik got up to follow, but the strong hands of Angootik stopped her.

'I think you had better leave him alone', he said.

'What do you think is the matter with him?' Ooramik asked.

Angootik answered, 'Reliving that tragedy again is a great burden.'

'I'll go to him', Putooktee said, and she went out.

Putooktee went out and found Kamik. She saw him staring at the sky, with tears in his eyes. Kamik heard her and turned.

'I am sorry to be like this', Kamik said. 'I should be happy to be alive.'

'I understand', Putooktee said. 'I'm sorry about your father and your friend. But life goes on.'

Kamik said, 'Life will never be the same without Father.'

'I realize that,' Putooktee said, 'but you have your

mother and the responsibility to look after her. And I hope you will move to Kikitajoak.'

Kamik looked squarely into Putooktee's eyes. 'This is the first time I ever saw a really pretty girl.'

'Thank you', Putooktee said. 'And I like you, Kamik.'

'You do?'

'Yes.'

Kamik moved closer. Putooktee stretched her arms to receive Kamik's arms. And he held her for a long time.

'Will you be my woman, Putooktee?' Kamik asked.

'Yes, I would willingly,' Putooktee said, 'but you must ask my father.'

'I will now.'

They went back inside the igloo. Kamik went to Angootik and said loudly, 'I am asking you to give me your daughter as my woman.' Everyone was surprised.

Angootik said, 'This is very sudden. Give me a few minutes to think.'

Netsiak stood up and said, 'The woman in question happens to be the woman who will belong to me someday.'

Kamik looked at Netsiak and said, 'Suppose we let Angootik and Putooktee decide that.'

Angootik finally said, 'In a situation like this, I can't make up my mind. I will leave the decision to Putooktee.'

Putooktee looked at Kamik and Netsiak. Then she said, 'I choose Kamik.'

Netsiak went over to Putooktee and said, 'But you have known him only one night.'

Putooktee said, 'I know that. And I have known you all my life, but I have never learned to love you. I'm sorry,

Netsiak, but my decision is final.'

Netsiak took Kamik by his shoulder and pushed him away violently and said, 'You don't think I'm giving up that easy, do you? I challenge you to fight to the death. And the winner will take Putooktee.'

'I am willing', Kamik said.

'Now wait', Angootik said. 'I'm in command here, and I say there will be no battle fought.'

'I'm sorry we ever found you alive', Netsiak said to Kamik.

And Kamik said, 'And I am sorry that you were born as a man and not as an animal.'

'That's enough', Angootik said. 'It is clear that my daughter has chosen Kamik to be her man, and that will be final. I'm not playing favourites with anybody, but I want my daughter to marry the man she loves.' He went

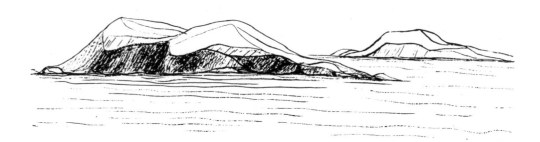

on, 'Now that everything is clear, Kamik and the rest of the people will have to move to Kikitajoak.'

'I guess we don't have much choice', Ooramik said. 'With the hunters gone, we will face many dangers.'

Kamik said, 'Yes. I think it is all for the best that we move to Kikitajoak.'

'But we will face great danger crossing the channel', Issa said.

Angootik said, 'That's true, but we have faced greater danger. We went through it once and we can do it again.' He went on, 'We have a long way to go. I guess we had better retire for the night.'

IT WAS WINDY AND COLD NEXT DAY as they travelled. The wind was high; the bitter cold wind bit on their faces. Kamik had been given a sled and dogs, and Ooramik and Putooktee were with him. Once he looked at Netsiak and saw hate in his eyes. He was sure Netsiak would try something to harm him and he would have to be on guard. Three sunrises later, they reached Kamik's home. Kamik saw the weeping widows of the hunters and their children, and the tears rolled down his face.

Next day all the people left for Kikitajoak. Kamik felt sad as he looked back at the empty camp he had grown up in and loved. Now he must start a new life in a totally strange country. But with Putooktee as his wife he knew that he would adjust to the new country and find happiness in that land. Only one thing lay in their path. The channel that never froze.

Two sunrises later they got to the edge of the channel. Before they started crossing, Angootik called everyone to his side. 'We must plan carefully', he said. 'Those who have children in their sleds will be in the middle. If anything happens to any of them, help will arrive from either side. I myself will lead the rest, with Kamik behind me. I will take Ooramik with me and Putooktee will be with Kamik.'

'What will we do if anything goes wrong?' Mittik asked.

Angootik answered, 'Those who are in danger must move fast, before they sink. And they will go to the nearest sleds if their dogs or sleds start to go down. And they must move fast, or they will go down with them.'

'Isn't there any other place less dangerous we could try to cross on?' Ooramik asked.

'I'm afraid not', Angootik answered. 'This is the only way.'

'What about us women?' Toogak asked. 'What can we do to help?'

Angootik answered, 'If you can, you can run alongside the sleds to reduce the weight of the load on the sleds. But watch your step all the way. Make sure the ice you are about to step on is solid enough to support your weight. And one more thing', he continued. 'I want the men to have their harpoons in their hands all the time. With your harpoons you must test the ice before you step on it, and those who are behind must follow in your steps.'

The time had come to cross. With Angootik in the lead, they started one by one. The men tested the ice before they stepped on it. Sometimes the harpoon went right through, indicating the ice was too thin to step on, and

79

they had to detour. Although it was cold they sweated, some of them with fear of sinking. Then without warning disaster struck.

Angootik saw his dogs starting to sink through the soft ice. Before he could say a word, he felt the ice under him giving away. He started yelling to Ooramik to get out of the sled. Too late. Ooramik went down with the sled and dogs, and disappeared quickly. Angootik, with water up to his neck, yelled, 'Not this way! Not this way! Go around. Don't go here.'

Kamik saw the whole thing. He saw Ooramik sink and disappear, and Angootik about to sink. Forgetting the danger, he ran to Angootik, with Putooktee right behind him. Then Kamik felt the ice under him starting to give away. Quickly he took one step back and tried to go around. Putooktee, seeing her father starting to sink, didn't stop. She went right on through the dangerous ice.

'Look out! You're starting to sink', yelled Kamik.

The warning came too late. Putooktee went through the ice. Kamik jumped and tried to reach her, but she had already disappeared. Kamik held onto the ice to stop his sinking and yelled for Putooktee. Angootik, too, had disappeared. Knowing they were beyond help, Kamik dragged himself out of the water. He turned and looked at the other sleds. They were out of danger, and some of the men were running toward him.

He heard Issa yell, 'Kamik! Quickly! This way, before you're carried away!'

But Kamik stood still. He didn't care. First he had lost his father. Now he had lost his mother and Putooktee. _and_ Life was not worth living any more. Kamik knew he could

80

her father, Angootik

still make it to safety on foot. Safety was not far, but still he did not move. *He is too grief stricken.*

HE WAS CARRIED OUT TO SEA and soon disappeared from the rest. He had waited until he was out of sight to do what he had to do. 'Before my father died, he said only dead people find everlasting peace. He said he was going where there was peace. And he said he would wait for me.' Kamik looked at the harpoon in his hands. Now the time had come. Now was the time to find peace, and to find the family and people he loved. He kneeled and put the tip of the harpoon to his throat. Suddenly he pushed it in. And, for the last time, the harpoon of the hunter made its kill.